Tax Planning For Forex Traders

Lee J Hadnum

IMPORTANT LEGAL NOTICES:

WealthProtectionReportTM
TAX GUIDE - "Tax Planning For Forex Traders"

Published by:
WealthProtectionReport.co.uk
Email: sales@wealthprotectionreport.co.uk

First Edition: January 2014

Copyright
Copyright © WealthProtectionReport.co.uk All rights reserved.

No part of this publication may be reproduced or transmitted in any form or by any means (electronically or mechanically, including photocopying, recording or storing it in any medium by electronic means) without the prior permission in writing of the copyright owner except in accordance with the provisions of the Copyright, Designs and Patents Act 1988 or under the terms of a licence issued by the Copyright Licensing Agency Ltd, 90 Tottenham Court Road, London, W1P 0LP. All applications for the written permission of the copyright owner to reproduce or transmit any part of this Tax Guide should be sent to the publisher.
Warning: Any unauthorised reproduction or transmission of any part of this Tax Guide may result in criminal prosecution and a civil claim for damages.

Trademarks
The logo "WealthProtectionReportTM" is a trademark of WealthProtectionReport.co.uk. All other logos, trademarks, names and logos in this Tax Guide may be trademarks of their respective owners.

DISCLAIMER

1. Please note that this tax guide is intended as general guidance only for individual readers and does NOT constitute accountancy, tax, legal, investment or other professional advice. WealthProtectionReport and the author accept no responsibility or liability for loss which may arise from reliance on information contained in this tax guide.

2. Please note that tax legislation, the law and practices by government and regulatory authorities (for example, HM Revenue and Customs) are constantly changing and the information contained in this tax guide is only correct as at the date of publication. We therefore recommend that for accountancy, tax, investment or other professional advice, you consult a suitably qualified accountant, tax specialist, independent financial adviser, or other professional adviser. Please also note that your personal circumstances may vary from the general examples given in this tax guide and your professional adviser will be able to give specific advice based on your personal circumstances.

3. This tax guide covers UK taxation mainly and any references to 'tax' or 'taxation' in this tax guide, unless the contrary is expressly stated, are to UK taxation only. Please note that references to the 'UK' do not include the Channel Islands or the Isle of Man. Addressing all foreign tax implications is beyond the scope of this tax guide.

4. Whilst in an effort to be helpful, this tax guide may refer to general guidance on matters other than UK taxation, WealthProtectionReport and the author are not experts in these matters and do not accept any responsibility or liability for loss which may arise from reliance on such information contained in this tax guide.

CONTENTS

1. Trading or Investing in Forex
2. National Insurance For Forex Traders
3. Top Tax Deductions
4. Maximising Home Deductions
5. CGT Matching Rules For Forex Investors
6. Making The Most Of Capital Losses
7. Deferring CGT On Forex Gains
8. Income Splitting To Reduce Tax
9. Common Forex Q&A's
10. Avoiding The 45% Rate of Income Tax
11. Using a UK Company For Forex Investing/Trading
12. Using An Existing Company
13. Non Residence And Forex Tax
14. Tax Planning If You Plan To Become Non Resident In The Future
15. Establishing Treaty Residence Overseas
16. When You Can Benefit From Offshore Forex
17. Using An Offshore Broker For Forex Trading Or Investing
18. Making The Most Of Non Residence

19　Using An Offshore Company For Forex Trading Or Investing
20　Using An Offshore Foundation For Forex Trading Or Investing

ABOUT THE AUTHOR

Lee Hadnum LLB ACA CTA is a trading tax specialist. He is a Chartered Accountant and Chartered Tax Adviser and is the Editor of the popular tax planning website:

www.wealthprotectionreport.co.uk

Lee is also the author of a number of best selling tax planning books including:

- **Tax Planning Techniques Of The Rich & Famous** - Essential reading for anyone who wants to use the same tax planning techniques as the most successful Entrepreneurs, large corporations and celebrities

- **The Worlds Best Tax Havens** – 220 page book looking at the worlds best offshore jurisdictions in detail

- **Non Resident & Offshore Tax Planning** – Offshore tax planning for UK residents or anyone looking to purchase UK property or trade in the UK. A comprehensive guide.

- **Tax Planning With Offshore Companies & Trusts: The A-Z Guide** - Detailed analysis of when and how you can use offshore companies and trusts to reduce your UK taxes

- **Tax Planning For Company Owners** – How company owners can reduce income tax, corporation tax and NICs

- **How To Avoid CGT In 2013/2014** – Tax planning for anyone looking to reduce UK capital gains tax

- **Buy To Let Tax Planning** – How property investors can reduce income tax, CGT and inheritance tax

- **Asset Protection Handbook** – Looks at strategies to ringfence your assets in today's increasing litigious climate

- **Working Overseas Guide** – Comprehensive analysis of how you can save tax when working overseas

- **Double Tax Treaty Planning** – How you can use double tax treaties to reduce UK taxes

1. WHAT IS AN EXCLUDED PROPERTY TRUST?

Anyone new to trading or investing in forex will want to know how they'll be taxed in the UK on any profits or gains they make, and also on how they'll get tax relief for any losses.

The key initial issue for anyone involved in buying or selling forex will be whether they are taxed as a trader or investor.

You may describe yourself informally as being a forex trader but for tax purposes you may well still be an investor. This can have a massive impact on your tax position.

HMRC will look at 'badges of trade' to determine whether your activity is trading or investment in nature.

There is no straight answer as regards to buying and selling forex, however, we shall first explain the rules in general.

These principles have been established through a number of judicial decisions, where there has been some doubt as to whether a series of transactions (or in some cases one transaction) can be defined as amounting to a 'trading activity'.

Motive

This is crucial, although it is also often the most difficult area to actually prove to the Revenues satisfaction.

If the Revenue believe that the motive in buying and selling the forex was the realisation of profit, this would be a significant factor when deciding whether to treat the transaction as trading.

Clearly this is a vague notion and in practice can be difficult to rely on and they will not rely solely on your own opinion of your intention, rather they look at the facts of the transaction to ascertain the 'true position'. Matters to be considered will include:

- whether the forex purchase is an isolated event. The test that HMRC will apply is whether the operations involved in the transaction are of the same kind or character, and carried on in the same way as other typical forex traders
- whether you have any other employment/self employment or whether this is your sole 'occupation'
- whether on the sale of the forex, you reinvest the proceeds in buying more currency

The actual transaction

They will also look at the circumstances of the actual transaction to identify whether any aspect of this indicates a trading motive.

In particular they will assess:

- The length of time between the purchase of the forex and the disposal
- The frequency of the forex transactions, ie the number of purchases and disposals you enter into. This will be a KEY factor that will be considered in practice. They will be looking for evidence of a 'continuous and habitual' activity, ie regular purchases and disposals of forex as opposed to infrequent and sporadic purchases and disposals
- What was the cause of the sale? The sale of the forex for an 'emergency' may make the likelihood of the transaction being trading less likely.
- Whether any finance was obtained for the purchase.

Whilst the above factors are all considered , the general view of the Revenue is that the purchase would usually be considered investment assets.

What if Forex is my only source of income?

Establishing when you are and aren't a forex trader is not straightforward though. In particular one of the questions we're frequently asked is whether if forex income is your only income this will make you a trader?

Just because it's you only 'income' would not automatically make it trading income. The whole nature of your activity would need to be assessed. The general rule with forex activities just as shares, derivatives and other financial assets is that you are an investor.

There would need to be an organised trading operation before you'd be classed as a trader. In the case of an individual (ie not a company) this is more difficult to apply.

The fact that the forex income is your only income would not therefore mean anything by itself. You could for instance have no other income but earn generous profits from a minimal number of trades per week and essentially be 'lucky' with your investments.

By contrast you could have another occupation, trade frequently with sophisticated risk management and a commercial set up and have a better chance of being classed as a trader.

Currency Derivatives

Currency derivatives fall into various categories including:

- Forward currency contracts which is an agreement to buy or sell currency at a fixed price at a fixed date.
- Currency options where the holder has the right, to buy or sell a fixed amount of currency at a fixed price.
- Currency swaps where parties effectively swap a loan in a foreign currency for a loan of equivalent amount in sterling.
- Currency CFD's where the CFD holder can take either a long or short position on the future rate of exchange between two currencies.

In determining how these are taxed you'll need to initially go back to basics and look at what the purpose of the derivative is.
You'll need to assess:

- Whether it's ancillary to a trading transaction - if it is any profit or loss would be assessed as profit or loss arising from a trade
- If not, it is ancillary to a capital transaction? If it is any gain or loss would be a capital gain or loss
- If it's not ancillary to anything else is it a trading transaction it's

own right? If it is again any profit or loss would be assessed as profit or loss arising from a trade
- If it's not a trading transaction in its own right it'll be an investment transaction and subject to the CGT rules.

Ancillary transactions

The currency derivative will be ancillary to another transaction usually if you use it as a form of hedging. So if you use it to hedge risks in a trading business it will be ancillary to trading purposes.

Capital treatment is the opposite and will apply when you use the derivative to hedge the exchange risks when you're buying a capital assets (eg land).

Example

Rolf intends to purchase a property overseas. To reduce the risk of the exchange rate going against him he firstly purchases a foreign currency future in advance of the purchase of the property denominated in that currency, The future is clearly ancillary to the capital acquisition of the property and any gain on the currency future would be assessed to capital gains tax.

The currency future would be on a trading account if Rolf was an importer of electronics from Japan and was worried about the movements in the Yen. Any gain on a Yen derivative would be taxed as part of his trading profits.

Currency derivatives not ancillary?

If currency derivatives aren't ancillary such as where you by them as part of a trading strategy in their own right then you'll need to look at the overall intention and frequency of purchases. HMRC would look to assess you on the badges of trade just as any other trader to determine whether you're a trader or investor. If you are a trader any profits would be taxed as income.

Should you be an investor or trader?

If you buy and sell shares or any other type of stock market security the default position for most people is that you'll be taxed as a share investor. Essentially this means that any profits you make will be subject to UK CGT.

You'll also be able to claim the various CGT reliefs such as the annual exemption. Any losses you make on shares will be capital losses and offset against any future gains you may realise (from shares or other assets).

This is pretty well known and will apply automatically to most share speculators.

The alternative is to be classed as a share trader. Why would you want to get classed as a share trader?

Well there are a number reasons why share trader status could be beneficial.

Firstly, the treatment of any losses you incur is much more flexible. So rather than just being carried forward and offset against any more capital gains, you can actually offset the losses against any other income for the tax year of the loss. You could therefore offset the loss against any employment income, interest income or trading income you may have. If you've suffered a tax deduction at source eg for salary payments or interest receipts, you'll be looking to get a tax refund from the taxman.

The loss relief rules have been enhanced so that trading losses can be carried back for up to 3 years. So if you realised a large loss of shares and argued you were a trader you could look to offset these against other income in the previous 3 years. Other income includes:

- Investment income
- Rental income
- Employment income
- Trading income

The loss that can be carried back 1 year is unlimited but the loss that can go back to years 2 and 3 is capped at £50,000.

Secondly, you'll get a much wider deduction for expenses.

For CGT purposes, you'll only be able to deduct the cost of the shares along with any incidental expenses of acquisition/disposal (eg stamp duty, trading fees). However, a share trader is taxed just as any other business. So, you can claim for any expenses you incur 'wholly and exclusively' for the purposes of the share trading.

This is basically a limitless deduction and there are a whole manner of things you can claim for. Here's some examples:

- Subscriptions to investment magazines
- Subscriptions to online trading facilities
- Investment books
- Share evaluation software
- Costs of a home office
- Capital allowances for capital expenditure (eg computers)
- Salary for any employees
- Office expenses such as paper, pens etc

Of course, it's not all benefits, a share trader may need to pay NIC, although this would be reduced if you already have a job and pay NIC's. In addition you won't get any of the CGT reliefs (ie mainly the annual exemption,) and will pay income tax.

It's being subject to income tax, rather than CGT that is the big drawback of share trading status. You'll then be taxed at 20% or 40%/45% compared to just 18% or 28% if you were subject to CGT. You'll also lose the annual CGT exemption of £10,900 for 2013/2014.

Traders have a wider expense/deduction offset and are classed as self employed. This means if they had no other income they'd also need to account for national insurance (class 2 at around £2.50 per week) and class 4 at 9% on profits above the primary threshold).

So essentially if you're a basic rate tax payer it's the difference between 18% CGT and 29% income tax and NIC. If you're a higher rate taxpayer the rate difference is 42% v 28%. There's also the allowances/expenses etc to take into account.

Whether the benefits of more flexible losses and increased expense deductions would outweigh the loss of CGT reliefs would depend on your particular circumstances.

General rule – no expenses

If there are no significant expenses there is no tax benefit to be derived from forex trader status. The fores investor comes out on top thanks to the 18% and 28% rates of CGT, the annual CGT exemption and the fact that no national insurance is payable.

But what if there are significant costs, such as software, rent and subscriptions? Does this make trader classification more appealing?

An individual earning profits of £100,000 would pay capital gains tax of £21,747 or income tax and national insurance of £34,165. Therefore, in order to make share trader treatment worthwhile from a tax perspective, tax savings of over £12,418 would need to be achieved, which would require a large level of tax deductible costs.

2. NIC FOR FOREX TRADERS

One of the big advantages that forex investors have over forex traders is that they aren't subject to national insurance.

National insurance is paid by employees, self employed individuals and also companies that pay salary to employees.
It's effectively another tax to pay and for anyone within the basic rate band it's a further tax charge at 9%. Above the higher rate level, NIC is payable at 2%.

So when you're looking at the effective tax rate faced by share, forex traders you need to take into account both:

Income tax which is payable at 20% within the basic rate band and 40% above it, and

National insurance which is a further 9% or 2%

The net effect is an effective tax rate of 29% for basic rate taxpayers and 42% for higher rate taxpayers.

If you earn above £150,000 you would suffer an effective tax rate of 47%.

Investors by contrast do not suffer any national insurance and are just subject to the flat 18% or 28% rate of CGT.

As such purely in terms of the tax rates, forex investors have a significant advantage over forex traders.

How much NIC is payable?

A self employed forex trader would be required to pay the following national insurance contributions:

- Class 2 contributions - these are fixed at £2.70 per week for the 2013/2014 tax year. This equates to an Annual bill: £140
- Class 4 contributions - 9% on profits between £7,755 and £41,450 and 2% on profits above the £41,450.

The profits taken into account are the taxable profits that you make from the shares. Therefore you'll be looking at the annual accounts which should show the proceeds of the share disposals and the cost of the shares sold, less any administrative expenses.

This table calculates the NIC bill on varying profit levels:

NICs for Traders	
Profits	National Insurance
£	£
10,000	342
20,000	1,242
30,000	2,142
40,000	3,042
50,000	3,343
60,000	3,543
70,000	3,743
80,000	3,943
90,000	4,143
100,000	4,343
130,000	4,943
150,000	5,343
180,000	5,943
200,000	6,343

You'll see how the national insurance bill increases quite rapidly up to profits of £40,000, then the increases level off as the 9% rate is replaced by the additional 2% rate.

Here's an example showing how the figures are calculated:

Sharon trades forex and generates profits of £60,000 per year. Her NIC would be calculated as:

£41,450 - £7,755 @ 9% = £3,032.55
£60,000 - £41,450 @ 2% = £371.00

Class 4 national insurance = £3,403
Class 2 national insurance = £140

Total national insurance £3,543

Trading income

As stated above NIC applies to trading income of share/forex/derivative traders. However all of the above assumes that the trader had no other income that was subject to NIC. Therefore it assumes for instance that they may just have the trading income and any other income was interest or rental income and exempt from NIC.

What about a forex trader who had a paid employment? In this case they could be potentially double charged to NIC as they'd pay NIC on their employment income as well as on their trading income.

The upper earnings limit of £41.450 is supposed to be the maximum income level charged at 9%. An employee though could be charged at 12% up to £41,450 on their employment income and 9% on another £41,450 of trading income.

In this case there are specific provisions that apply. To prevent yourself being charged to NIC twice you can either apply for a deferment before the tax year starts or a refund once the final liability has been calculated.

You may be able to defer payment of Class 4 (and Class 2) contributions if you expect to be both employed and self-employed during the tax year and:

- your earnings as an employee are likely to be substantial and
- your total National Insurance contributions liability will be over the maximum by more than £10.

Therefore for any traders who have another employment in which they are higher rate taxpayers they should be looking at a deferment application to avoid the Class 4 NIC's

Using a company to avoid NIC

If you are a trader a relatively simple method to avoid NIC would be to use a company to carry out your trade. In this case the company would not pay NIC on its profits and provided you extracted cash from the company by way of a low salary (below the lower limit) with the remainder as dividends you could completely avoid NIC on trading income. Of course there is much more to using a company than this and we've looked at the tax implications of using a company in other chapters.

3. TOP TAX DEDUCTIONS

If you're carrying out a trade as a forex trader you'll be assessed to income tax on the profits you make from buying and selling forex.

You can however deduct any expenses you incur carrying out your trade. The two main caveats to this are:

- It needs to be 'revenue' expenditure and not capital expenditure
- it needs to be incurred wholly & exclusively for the purposes of the forex trade

Revenue v capital

What is revenue and what is capital can be a difficult distinction to make but it's important for tax (and accounting purposes). Revenue expenditure goes through the P&L (reducing profits) whereas capital goes to balance sheet (and doesn't directly reduce profits).

The whole point of the distinction is to ensure that expenditure is matched with the year that you get the benefits. So as a general rule if expenditure is for the enduring benefit of the trade there's a good chance its capital in nature. The kind of things that this may include are a computer or specialist forex software that you buy.

Wholly & exclusively

You need to also ensure that expenses are incurred wholly & exclusively for the purposes of the forex trade and not for personal purposes or to benefit another trade.

Some of the top tax deductions for forex traders

To give you an idea here's some of the top tax deductions:

- Subscriptions to forex periodicals or planning websites
- Monthly forex charting services
- Books on forex planning
- If you use an office at home a share of the costs of running your home (see next chapter)
- Dealing or other advisory fees
- Interest charges on finance for the forex trade
- Bank charges
- Capital allowances on a computer used for the trade. Note that although a computer is a capital asset you can get tax relief via the capital allowance provisions. These can provide for a 100% tax relief on the cost of a computer.
- Cost of broadband/telephone line

If you share a line for personal and your forex trading use you'll need to apportion the cost between the two for tax purposes. If you have a separate line purely for forex trading the full cost would be allowable.

- Forex data feeding eg Infotecnet

4. MAXIMISING HOME DEDUCTIONS

Most forex traders trade from their home. As you'll be looking to reduce your income tax charge as much as possible ensuring that you claim all the expenses you are able to, is at the start of any effective tax planning strategy.

This applies to forex traders just as for other traders.

If you're carrying out a trade from your home you'll be entitled to claim a proportion of the costs of your home. The basis of the claim arises from the tax rule that permits you to deduct any expenses that you incur 'wholly & exclusively' for the purposes of a trade. In practice this is watered down so that where part of an expense relates to business it is claimed (and usually accepted) as a tax deductible expenses. Therefore a 'use of home' claim is possible as long as some work is carried out at home.

Forex Traders v Investors

You'll only be able to claim a share of the costs of running your home if you're a forex trader. If you're an investor the only expenses you'll be able to offset will the incidental expenses of acquisition & disposal (commission, stamp duty etc).

How Do I Get The Deduction?

Traders will need to prepare accounts and if they don't do so would need to prepare accounts for tax purposes anyway. When preparing the accounts you would include the expenses as a deduction from the profits.

How Much Can You Claim?

Claims should be based on the proportionate use of the property for the trade. There are many possible methods for calculating the business   proportion.

The main factors to consider are time and space: how much space is set aside for business use and how much time is spent on business.

In practice, the most popular method is to simply take the number of rooms used for the trade as a proportion of the total number of rooms in the house. Hallways, bathrooms and kitchens are excluded from the calculation.

So given that most traders will use just the one room for trading if a house had three bedrooms, a living room, a dining room, two bathrooms and a kitchen, we can ignore the bathrooms and the kitchen. This leaves five rooms for the purpose of our calculation, meaning that we can claim one fifth of the household costs.

This is the easiest option and will be the best option for many. However there are other options. You could for instance base it on floor space if the room that was used for trading was the largest room in the house.

Private use

When there is some private use of a room used for forex trading, you will need to restrict your claim.

If for instance you have a bedroom that you have your computer and use this to carry out your online trading you'll need to pro-rate the expenses between the private use and trading use.

For instance if you slept in it for 8 hours a night and then used it for 7 hours work your business use of that room would be 7/15 or around 47%.

It's also worthwhile noting that if there is any wasted space in house it's worthwhile using this primarily for trading use. This will then significantly increase the business use proportion and therefore the expense deduction.

Protect the CGT exemption

The CGT exemption which you usually get when you sell your home is restricted if part of the house has been used exclusively for trading. However, as long as there is some private use of each room in the house, no matter how small, your CGT relief is safe.

You can also compensate for a small amount of private use of your 'trading room' with a small element of trading use in another room, thus restoring your income tax deduction with no loss of CGT relief.

What home expenses can forex traders claim for?

There are lots of expenses that traders can claim for. Some of the main ones are:

- Mortgage interest
- Council tax
- Water rates
- Repairs and maintenance
- Building and contents insurance
- Electricity
- Gas, oil or other heating costs
- Cleaning
- Telephone and internet costs
- General repairs and maintenance
- Costs which are specific to an area used for work may be claimed in full -- subject to any reduction required for partial private use of that area.

Bear in mind that this is in addition to any expenses that relate specifically to forex trading (trading software, subscriptions etc)

You can also vary the deduction according to the business use. So in the case of the internet for instance, if you use this primarily for online trading (researching, executing trades, online trading forums etc) you could claim a deduction for internet costs at 80 or 90% of the total costs.

Capital allowances

You can also claim capital allowances on any furniture and equipment used for forex trading. You can currently get immediate 100% relief on expenditure of up to £250,000 a year (subject to a reduction for any private use). So again buying a computer used solely for trading would qualify for 100% tax relief (meaning the cost would reduce your taxable profits.

Therefore traders can claim some substantial tax deductions for the expenses of running their home.

Tax relief on Brokers fees

Obtaining tax relief for your expenses is one of the basic elements of any tax planning strategy.

If you're a forex investor (as opposed to a trader) you'll be subject to capital gains tax on any profits that you make when you buy and sell forex.

The costs that you can deduct are specified in the capital gains tax legislation. In particular you will only be able to deduct:

- The cost of the shares etc
- Any incidental costs of buying and selling them

It's this latter category that you'll be particularly concerned with to see if you can squeeze out any extra tax deductions. The capital gains tax legislation states that allowable incidental costs are limited to:

- fees, commission or remuneration paid for the professional services of any:

-surveyor/valuer/auctioneer
-accountant
-legal adviser
- costs of transfer or conveyance (including Stamp Duty)
- costs of advertising to find a buyer or seller
- costs reasonably incurred in making any valuation or apportionment required for the purposes of the Capital Gains Tax computation.

How does this apply to forex investors?

HMRC will only allow a deduction for fees paid to a professional adviser if the fees are directly referable to the cost of acquiring or disposing of each particular investment.

If the fees relate to advice about the general state of markets or the prospects of particular forms of investment or the management of a portfolio, they would not be allowable for capital gains tax purposes.

What about my accountants fees?

Accountant's fees are allowable only to the extent that they relate to:

- the ascertainment of market value of the assets or
- any apportionment for the purposes of the capital gains tax calculation. For most forex investors this will be very rare (unless for instance you transferred investments to a family member or had acquired them before March 1982) and allowable accountancy fees will therefore be low.

You won't be allowed a deduction for subscriptions for periodicals or for publications by analysts, stockbrokers or other professional advisers. The expenditure listed above will the only expenditure you can deduct.

So it's important that any professional fees are clearly split between the actual dealing costs and advisory fees. The former will qualify for a CGT deduction.

Traders

As we've seen if you're a forex trader though you aren't governed by these rules. You can deduct any expenses that you incur 'wholly & exclusively' for the purposes of buying and selling forex. So you'll get tax relief for all of the expenses above, plus plenty more.

Of course being a trader also means that you could be taxed at up to 47% as opposed to 28% if you're an investor, so you'd need to be very careful before simply swapping to trader status to obtain more expense deductions.

Having said that if you're paying income tax at the basic rate for instance the greater tax relief for expenses may lead to a lower tax bill than if you were an investor. However even with similar rates of tax a trader still had NIC and the loss of the annual CGT exemption to contend with.

5. CGT MATCHING RULES

Unless you're classed as a forex trader you'll be subject to capital gains tax on any gains made on buying & selling forex. This is because currency is a chargeable asset for capital gains tax purposes.

In particular it's important to note that forex is subject to the same rules of identification and pooling as shares and securities. These are commonly known as the 'matching rules' and apply so that you can determine what the base cost is of your currency for CGT purposes.

This is important as if you've bought Japanese Yen for instance over a lengthy period and then sold some of it you need to know which Yen acquisitions you have sold. Your capital gain could be significantly different depending on the exchange rate for the particular acquisition.

How the pooling rules work

There is a definite order in which acquisitions should be considered. When you sell forex you would look at your holding of that particular currency and match the disposals with:

- currency acquired on the date of disposal;
- currency acquired in the 30 days following the date of disposal ;
- currency in your currency pool

The first two matching rules are to prevent the bed and breakfasting of forex.

The currency pool

The currency pool means that all purchases are treated as a single pool, growing or diminishing as forex is acquired and disposed of. The allowable cost on a disposal will therefore represent a pro rating of the total costs of all the currency.

Note that this represents the position for periods after 5 April 2008. Before this date it was more complex.

Example

Bert acquired Forex as follows:

15 May 2003	$20,000	=	£10,000
27 June 2009	$40,000	=	£25,000
9 September 2013	$40,000	=	£30,000

He then sold $60,000 for £60,000.

Under the new rules the pool would contain all of the $ currency as follows:

Currency $100,000

Cost £65,000

On a disposal of $60,000 the base cost would be £39,000 (ie 60,000/100,000*£65,000)

This is a much simpler method of calculating gains and means that investors will simply add the cost of currency including any incidental costs such as dealing commission etc to the pool for calculating gains.

6. MAKING THE MOST OF CAPITAL LOSSES

If you dispose of forex for less than the original cost, a capital loss arises. The general rule is that a capital loss can be offset against capital gains you have made in the current tax year.

If you still have losses left over, these can be carried forward and offset against gains made in future tax years.

The important point to note is that losses incurred in a previous tax year are only used to reduce your current year's chargeable gains down to £10,900, the amount of the annual capital gains tax exemption.

This is good news because it prevents the annual CGT exemption from being wasted.

Example

Justin, a higher-rate taxpayer, made the following share transactions:

- April 6 2013 sold currency and suffered a loss of £10,000.
- July 1 2013 sold more currency and made a gain of £12,000.

The loss of £10,000 is offset against the gain of £12,000 (as these occurred in the same tax year), leaving a net gain of £2,000. The tax position would be as follows:

Gain	=	£12,000
Less:		
Loss	=	£10,000
Less:		
Annual		exemption
£10,900 but restricted to	=	£2,000
Taxable Gain	=	NIL

As no other gains occurred during the tax year, £8,900 of the annual exemption is effectively wasted. But if the loss of £10,000 was incurred in the previous tax year, and carried forward to the current 2013/2014 tax year, only £1,100 of the loss would be offset:

Gain	=	£12,000
Less:		
Loss	=	£1,100
Less:		
Annual exemption	=	£10,900
Gain	=	NIL

The remaining £8,900 of losses can be carried forward to the next tax year and potentially result in a tax saving of £2,492 (28% of £8,900).

Because losses carried forward are worth more than losses written off in the current tax year, the crucial question is, how do you ensure your losses are carried forward rather than used up in the current tax year?

Sell loss-making investments

One way of maximising the benefit is to sell currency standing at a loss in a year when you have no other capital gains.

Example

Bill has £12,000 profit showing on a holding of Yen and a £12,000 loss showing on a Dollar holding. If he sells them in the same tax year he will pay no capital gains tax but will also waste most of his annual CGT exemption. If instead he just sells Dollars he will make a loss of £12,000. This loss will be carried forward to the next tax year. Let's say in this next tax year he sells the Yen. The tax calculation will be as follows:

Gain =		£12,000
Less:		
Previous year's loss	=	£1,100
Less:		

Annual exemption = £10,900

Taxable Gain

NIL

And he still has £10,600 of losses to carry forward to future tax years!

Married Couples or Civil Partners

Another way of making the most of losses is to ensure that loss-making holdings are not owned jointly.

It often makes sense for married couples to own investments jointly so that they can make full use of two annual CGT exemptions. With losses the opposite is sometimes true. To ensure losses can be carried forward it often pays for only one spouse to own the investments.

Example

Bill and Wendy have £5,000 of profits showing on Yen and £5,000 of losses showing on Dollars. They want to dispose of both holdings in the current tax year. If they sell both, the gain from will be offset by the and no tax will be payable. However, they will also waste their annual capital gains tax exemptions.

If instead Bill owns and sells Yen plc and Wendy owns and sells the Dollars, Bill will not have to pay any tax because his gain will be covered by his annual CGT exemption. Wendy's £5,000 loss will be carried forward to future tax years.

Alternatively they could sell Bear plc now and Bull plc in the new tax year, just as in the previous example. This may have the same tax consequences but may not be a desirable investment strategy.

7. DEFERRING CGT ON FOREX GAINS

Investors often ask whether they can defer any capital gains that arise on forex, and if so how can they achieve this. In this article we look at some of the options for deferring capital gains for forex investors.

Rollover relief

Traditionally this is the key relief that most business owners use to defer capital gains. However applying it to forex investors is a non starter for a number of reasons:

- Firstly rollover relief is available to assets that are used for the purposes of a trade. If you're an investor this will clearly not apply.

- Even if you were a forex trader it wouldn't apply as the disposals then wouldn't be of 'assets', instead the forex etc would be classed as your stock.

In other words you wouldn't be holding the forex as investment assets that were used in your trade, the forex would actually be trading stock. The charge would then be to income tax on a disposal not CGT. As such no rollover relief would be due.

- Finally rollover relief is only due on various categories of 'qualifying assets'. As forex doesn't fall within this definition it wouldn't qualify in any case.

Therefore there's no prospect for a rollover relief claim to defer CGT on forex.

Gift relief

If you gift forex or transfer it at less than the market value you'll usually still be charged to CGT. In this case, the market value of the forex is likely to be used in the CGT calculation and for the purposes of calculating the gain (otherwise it would just be too easy to avoid CGT!).

Note that for shares there is also a provision that allows a form of deferral relief where a shares are gifted. It won't apply to all shares though and the main categories of shares that investors may qualify for gift relief on will therefore be shares listed on the AIM.

This would however not apply to forex.

Gift relief on transfer to a trust

As well as gift relief available on transfers of business assets, there's also a separate form of gift relief that applies on the transfer to a discretionary trust. This applies to all assets (including forex).

Although gift relief is still available on transfers to a trust there are now a number of exemptions to this, including where the trust is a settlor interested trust (generally if you, your spouse or children can benefit from the trust).

So unless you were planning on transferring to a trust which did not have you or your immediate family as beneficiaries you couldn't transfer forex to it and claim the CGT deferral.

EIS relief

This relief applies to all assets. So it doesn't matter what your gain has arisen from. Whether it's shares (in an investment or trading company), forex, derivatives or any other security, the gain would potentially qualify for the EIS deferral relief.

Provided you reinvest proceeds equivalent to the gain into shares that qualify under the EIS scheme you'll be able to defer the gain arising on the forex disposal until the EIS shares are eventually sold.

The Enterprise Investment Scheme ('EIS') offers a number of tax benefits to investors. The key tax benefits are:

- Income tax relief. This provides for a reduction in your income tax charge of 30% of the amount invested (up to £1,000,000)
- A capital gains tax exemption which allows EIS shares to be sold free of CGT when they qualify for income tax relief
- A deferral relief

It is this latter relief that can be particularly useful if you're looking to avoid CGT.

The deferral relief allows you to defer a capital gains tax charge on the disposal of any other assets, when you purchase EIS shares.

This means you can avoid paying CGT on forex investments providing you reinvest some of the proceeds into EIS shares.

Note that you don't have to reinvest all of the proceeds, To claim full EIS deferral relief you just need to reinvest an amount equal to the capital gain that arose. So if you sold forex for £200,000, to defer the CGT on this you'd need to reinvest the £200,000 into EIS shares.

Time limit

There is a time limit as you'd expect and you need to make any EIS investment within 12 months before and 36 months after the capital gain arose.

Deferral v Exemption

The EIS deferral claim though is only a deferral -- not an exemption. So if you sell forex investments at a gain of £100,000 and reinvest into EIS shares no CGT would be paid immediately, however, when you sell the EIS shares the £100,000 would then be taxed.
There are a few occasions when the deferred gain becomes chargeable. The main one is when the EIS shares are sold or no longer qualify as EIS shares.

Non Residence

The deferred gain can also be charged to CGT if you become non resident within (usually) three years.

If though you held onto the EIS shares for more than this, and then became non resident the deferral should become a full exemption.

This could be a useful method of avoiding CGT. Any gain on the EIS shares would also be free of CGT, however you'd need to make sure you were non resident for at least 6 complete tax years to avoid CGT being recharged on your return to the UK.

8. INCOME SPLITTING TO REDUCE TAX

Spreading ownership of assets between a husband and wife is one of the best ways of avoiding both income tax and capital gains tax. In this article we'll focus on the opportunities to save income tax.

The reason it's possible to split income is that spouses are treated as separate individuals for tax purposes BUT they are allowed to transfer assets between each other with no capital gains tax arising.

To benefit it's important that one of the spouses earns less income than the other. The best case scenario is where one spouse is a higher-rate or additional rate taxpayer (paying 25%/30.55% tax on dividend income and 40%/45% on rental profits and interest) and the other spouse earns no income at all.

Remember that, before tax has to be paid at the full rate, each UK resident individual is entitled to:

- A personal allowance, currently £9,440.
- A basic rate, currently 20% and 0% for dividend income.

The key is to make sure that your spouse's income tax personal allowance and lower tax rates are fully utilized.

In these circumstances, gifting assets to the low-income spouse will reap enormous tax savings. In certain circumstances there will be absolutely no tax payable at all!

Take the example of a married man who is a higher-rate taxpayer and realises gains on forex of £30,000. He would normally pay £5,348 in capital gains tax. If, however, his wife has no other gains, transferring half of the forex to her would lead to a combined tax bill on disposal of £2,296

And remember transferring assets to your spouse has absolutely no capital gains tax consequences.

9. COMMON FOREX TAX Q&A'S

Here's some of the most common tax Q&A's for forex traders/investors

What taxes will I be subject to?

This will depend on whether you're assessed as a forex trader or a forex investor.

A forex trader is subject to income tax and national insurance on the profits made.

A forex investor is subject to capital gains tax on any gains they make. Most individuals buying and selling forex will be taxed as an investor, so they'll pay CGT at the fixed 18% or 28% rate.

What is the difference between an investor and a trader?

Strictly speaking traders buy and sell for the purpose of making a profit whereas investors hold for investment returns. With financial assets though it's less straightforward than this and the general presumption is that you're an investor.

Do I pay tax on all my forex profits?

If you're an investor and assuming you have no other capital gains in the year (eg from selling other investments) then you'll be taxed on your forex gains above the annual CGT exemption (currently £10,900 in 2013/2014).

If you're a forex trader you're likely to already have used your personal allowance for income tax purposes. So your full profits would be subject to tax. The rate would depend on your level of total income (ie all your taxable income combined) but would be either 20% or 40% (if you're a higher rate taxpayer).

What if I make losses - how do I deal with these?

If you're an investor your losses will be capital losses and just carried forward for offset against your future capital gains.

If you're a forex trader then your losses could be offset against any other income in the same tax year or carried back against income in the previous tax year. This assumes that you are an 'active' trader for tax purposes and spend at least 10 hours per week on the forex trading.

Therefore forex trader status is attractive in terms of loss relief but less attractive if you make profits.

Will I need to complete a tax return?

Yes

What if I trade forex via a spread betting company?

Any gains you make will be free of UK tax and you won't have to enter details on the tax return. The corollary to this though is no relief for losses.

Is there any advantage to holding an account in another country?

Only if you are a forex investor and are also a non UK domiciliary claiming the remittance basis of tax. We look at this shortly.

Do I pay CGT on total profits on the account, or total profits withdrawn from the account? ie. does it become a capital gain when I make £100 profit or when you actually get it safely out of the account?

You generally make a capital gain when you sell the forex or otherwise close the transaction. Whether you leave your proceeds in your online account or not is irrelevant.

Could I save tax by using a company?

If profits are expected to be large there could be some tax advantages by making use of the company's lower rate of corporation tax for traders (ie 20% as opposed to 40% income tax). We look at this shortly.

What expenses can I deduct?

These are very strictly defined for forex investors. So basically just dealing costs. Forex traders could deduct any expenses related to the trade (eg subscriptions, periodicals, interest etc).

Could I avoid UK tax by moving abroad?

Yes, provided you structured both the UK and overseas aspects carefully (eg no tax in the overseas country of residence).

If I keep selling forex and reinvesting the profits into more forex can I avoid UK tax?

No. If you trade in your own name then you're taxed on the gains made irrespective of what you do with the proceeds. The exception to this is if you reinvested in shares that qualified under the EIS scheme. In this case you can defer CGT on the forex gain.

Can I spread the tax and reduce the overall tax due by sharing the account with my wife?

Yes if it's in both your names the gains should arise equally (assuming you're forex investors). The main advantage to this is that the annual CGT exemption is available to each of you (if not otherwise utilised). It would therefore potentially double tax relief to £21,800.

If I keep profits below the annual exemption do I still need to declare the gains?

Providing the gains are less than £10,900 and the total proceeds are less than £43,600 there would be no duty to disclose the forex gains.

Am I only charged to CGT when I withdraw cash from my account?

No I'm afraid not. You'll be charged to CGT when you make a disposal. In other words when you sell forex you need to calculate the gain/loss. Whether the cash is retained in your trading account or extracted is irrelevant – unless you are a non UK domiciliary who claims the remittance basis and hold cash in an overseas account.

10. AVOIDING THE 45% RATE OF INCOME TAX

As from April 2013 the tax rates are now:

- 20% tax for income within the basic rate band (ie > £32,010)).
- 40% tax for income in the higher rate band but below the new super tax band (for example, £32,010 - £150,000) .
- 45% tax for income above £150,000.

So whilst forex traders would be potentially subject to the new 45% rate of income tax, investors wouldn't - they would still be taxed at

28%. The differences in the tax rates are huge. In fact traders would face a higher tax rate than this as they would also need to take into account:

- The loss of the personal allowance if their income exceeds £100,000, and
- The rise in national insurance after April 2011, which increases to 2% for profits above the upper earnings threshold

So when you take into account the 45% tax rate & NIC you'd have a tax rate of 47%. When you also take into account the loss of the personal allowance the effective tax rate would be much more.

Using a company for your trades

If you're a forex trader facing an effective tax rate of well over 45% you could consider using a company to carry out the trades.

When you you look at the position of a company, it looks very favourable when compared to individuals.

The key issue is that the small company rate of corporation tax is currently 20%. When compared to a 40% or 45% rate of income tax this looks very attractive. Trading income would also be subject to NIC within the basic rate band, whereas company income wouldn't.

Of course this assumes that no profits are extracted from the company. If profits are extracted from the company there would then be an income tax charge. Many company users though would look to extract minimal cash from the company and benefit from the lower rate of corporation tax in the company.

Using a company would therefore be a simple option to avoiding the 45% income tax charge.

For many traders this can prove invaluable as halving their tax bill allows more cash for reinvestment, and hopefully maximizing returns in the long run. Of course cash does need to be extracted at some point. Fortunately there are a number of options. You could just extract cash as a dividend. If this was substantial the downside to this is that it would then be subject to the new 'super tax at 30.55%.

Better options to extract the cash include:

- Becoming non UK resident and extracting cash as a dividend free of UK income tax
- Becoming non UK resident and extracting cash as a capital distribution.

This would be free of UK capital gains tax providing the shareholder was non UK resident for at least 6 complete tax years.

- Simply extracting as a capital distribution.

A capital distribution is subject to CGT as opposed to income tax. In order to extract cash as capital rather than income the company would need to be wound up. If this applied, the cash received would be treated as disposal proceeds for a disposal of the shares.

The gain would then be taxed at 28% (ie CGT) as opposed to income tax (at rates up to 45%).

Of course the profits would have already suffered corporation tax (eg at 20%) however in many cases it's still substantially less than income tax and national insurance (for traders).

Who can benefit from using a company

Using a company to avoid the 45% rate of income tax can be beneficial for forex traders.

It's important though that you are classed as a trader and not an investor. If you can get yourself classed as an investor you should file on this basis. The 28% rate of personal CGT would mean that the tax payable would usually be significantly less than for investors using a company. If an investor used a company they would be likely to be subject to the 23% rate of corporation tax, which when added to the tax charge on extraction of funds from the company would substantially increase the tax bill.

It would generally only be if there were either substantial expenses to offset, you were planning on extracting very little cash from the company or if you were to invest via an existing trading company that a company may begin to rival personal investment for an investor.

Even then it can be very close and you should carefully weigh up the two options.

So just for traders?

Generally yes. You wouldn't want to 'shoot yourself in the foot' and form a company to trade from unless you're certain that HMRC would class you as a trader. So unless the position is very clear it may be advisable to wait for HMRC to rule on your status. You could then incorporate your business into a company at a later date.

Entrepreneurs Relief

In principle if the extraction is from a trading company Entrepreneurs Relief could reduce the rate of CGT from 28% to 10% on gains within the £10,000,000 allowance. However in practice if you built up significant cash reserves in the business any disposal or transfer of shares in the company could be 'penalized' as the shares may not qualify for Entrepreneurs Relief. This is because the Entrepreneurs Relief provisions don't count a company as a trading company if it has substantial non-trading assets or income.

Substantial in this context is taken to mean at least 20% of net assets or income. The Revenue will consider any form of non trading asset for this purposes including property held in a company which is let (eg old business premises) as well as surplus cash not required for the purposes of the trade.

Therefore anyone looking to maximise the benefit of the companies retained profits may have suffered a tax penalty in the future.

As such if a large amount of cash was generated in a company the best way to extract it if you were a UK resident would be to liquidate and pay a capital distribution. As above though the Revenue could then consider whether the company truly is a trading company for the purposes of Entrepreneurs Relief.

Even if Entrepreneurs Relief wasn't due, the rate of CGT at 28% is still substantially less than the income tax rate.

Pre liquidation dividend?

It's worthwhile bearing in mind that if there is no other income in the tax year of liquidation it makes sense to extract cash up to the basic rate band as a dividend. This will be free of income tax for the shareholders and reduce the future capital gain on the shares.

11. USING A COMPANY FOR FOREX INVESTING/TRADING

If you're considering using a company to hold forex you need to be aware of the close investment company rules.

It's important to note that these rules only apply to investment companies not trading companies. So if you're classed as a forex trader you won't be subject to these rules. If the company is forex investor you'll certainly need to consider them.

How do the close investment company provisions apply?

Investment companies are subject to different rules from trading companies. Many of the reliefs available to trading companies, such as Entrepreneurs Relief, rollover relief, and business property relief are NOT usually extended to investment companies.

As well as these specific provisions, there are also the Close Investment Company (CIC) provisions which apply to investment companies that are also 'close companies'.

The result of being classed as a CIC is that the lower rates of corporation tax are not available. Instead the company must pay tax at the 23% rate, irrespective of the level of profits.

Therefore, it's important that you know exactly what a close investment company is and when a company will fall within the definition. It should be noted however that the main rate will fall to 20% in the future in any case which will then equalise the position.

What is a Close Investment Company (CIC)?

First of all we must explain what a 'close company' is. In practice almost all small owner-managed companies are 'close companies'.

A close company is, generally speaking, any company that is controlled by:

- Its directors (including connected persons).
- Five or fewer participators. 'Participators' are generally shareholders, although this is a potentially wide term and can include loan creditors for a non-commercial loan.

Most companies are controlled by their directors and have fewer than five shareholders.

It's not a problem for a trading company to be classified as a close company. However, close companies that are also investment companies are specifically targeted. Just to make matters more confusing, the tax legislation defines a close investment company in the negative. A company will be a close investment company unless it exists for one or more of the following purposes:

- Carrying on a trade or trades on a commercial basis.
- Making investments in land for letting to unconnected persons.
- Acting as a holding company, in other words holding shares in companies within a trading/property investment group.
- Co-ordinating the administration of two or more group companies involved in trading/property investment activities.

You'll notice that there is a let out for property investment companies... but there is no such let out for forex investment companies. It is therefore likely that unless a company dealing forex can be classed as a trading company, it will be a close investment company and pay corporation tax at 23%.

Other Tax Consequences of Using a Company

There are other tax consequences of using a company. One of the key tax consequences is the loss of the annual capital gains tax exemption - £10,900 in the case of unmarried individuals and £21,800 if you're married and both own investments.

For the very small forex investor the loss of this exemption rules out using a company to buy and sell forex - no matter what advantages a company may offer, loss of the annual CGT allowance makes the whole exercise a waste of time.

The second point to note is the extra administrative burden of running a company. The rules governing the preparation of company accounts are stringent so you'll need to employ the services of an accountant - this all eats away at the tax savings you would otherwise have enjoyed.

Thirdly, companies cannot use the 18% rate of CGT that individuals are entitled to.

Summary

The odds are stacked against the use of a company for forex investment activities due to:

- The close investment company provisions
- The loss of the annual CGT exemption
- The loss of 18% CGT rate for basic rate taxpayers, and
- The extra admin burden placed on company owners.

As a general rule, forex investment activities are taxed most favourably when the shares are held personally rather than through a company. It's the CIC provisions that do the real damage, resulting in a massive 23% tax charge before the profits are even extracted. When compared to the 18% rate of CGT that basic rate investors pay this is a significant disadvantage. If you're a higher rate taxpayer you'd pay CGT at 28%. Although this is at a higher rate than the 23% corporation tax charge, this ignores the effect of extracting profits.

If you were to extract any profits from the company the 25% effective tax charge on dividends would easily outweigh the benefit.

It's only really if you're a trader or if there are other exceptional circumstances.

The main attractions in terms of using a company are:

- the 20% rate of corporation tax on profits up to £300,000 and
- the ability to retain profits without incurring a further income tax charge

Whether you can use these to reduce your UK tax burden will depend on your particular situation.

Traders

If you're a forex trader and are subject to income tax on your profits you could see a big advantage from using a company.

There are special provisions which apply to determine how forex is taxed in a company, however if the forex transactions are entered into as trading transaction they'll be taxed as trading receipts.

If you're subject to higher rate income tax as an individual you'd be paying 40% income tax personally (plus 2% NIC). Even if you're a basic rate payer you'd pay income tax at 20% and also have an 9% NIC liability. If your forex profits are above £150,000 per year you'd pay income tax at 45%.

By using a company you can eliminate your NIC bill and fix your tax rate at 20%.

This assumes that you don't extract any profits from the company, or if you do any extractions are within the basic rate tax band.

Potentially saving you tax & NIC on your profits this provides much more capital to reinvest for your trades.

Of course there will come a point when you want to extract your cash and it's at this point that you'll need to consider your UK income tax position.

The tax rate on dividends from your company will be an effective 25% if you're a higher rate taxpayer, 30.55% if you're in the additional rate and 0% if not. So ideally you want to make sure you extract cash within your basic rate tax band. This is around £41,500 so if you have limited other income you could extract cash up to this with no further tax to pay.

You could also consider bringing in your wife (or civil partner) as a shareholder and extracting cash within their basic rate tax band as well.

Another option could be to leave the UK and extract cash from the company free of UK income tax as a non UK resident.

Provided you can extract cash at a minimal tax cost the company can prove to be very effective in reducing your tax burden if you're a financial trader. Crucially using a company can also make it more likely that you'll be classed as a trader - if that is what you want!

12. USING AN EXISTING COMPANY FOR FOREX TRADING

Anyone with an existing trading or investment company may be considering carrying out their forex activities via the company. The key reason for this is often to avoid having to extract cash from the company with which to invest. By using the company's own funds you avoid the income tax charge on the extraction of the cash (which for a higher rate taxpayer would be at an effective 25% or 30.55% if your income extracted £150,000).

If you do use the company though it's important to realise that there can be a number of differences to how the forex is taxed when compared with if you invested in your own name.

Forex trading through a company

If you're trading in forex though the company it will be taxed on the forex as trading income just as with the other trading income of the company.

The forex trade would be regarded as a separate trade for tax purposes. So if for instance your other trade carried out via the company was publishing, you'd have two trades (one of forex trading & the other publishing).

You would need to 'stream' the profits from the two trades so that they were separately calculated. This is important as expenses of the forex trade could only be offset against forex income.

In addition if one of the trades incurred a loss in an accounting period this could be offset against the other income of the company (eg publishing profits). However if the loss was not fully utilised any excess that was carried forward would only be offset against future profits of the loss making trade (eg the future forex profits).
If you're a forex trader using the company can be attractive:

- You would avoid the income tax on extraction of funds to trade personally
- You could avoid any NIC charges
- You'd potentially be subject to income tax at 40% if you traded in your own name, however most small companies would pay tax at 20%.
- Forex losses can be offset against other company income/capital gains
- Provided you retained cash within the company or extracted within your basic rate tax band there would be no tax charge on extraction.

Of course if you were looking at simply extracting all of the forex profits from the company the company route would offer limited advantages as it would then be taxed at 20% in the company and 25% (if you're a higher rate taxpayer) on you personally. It's only where some or all of the profits are retained in the company that using a company could be a good option.

Forex investors

The treatment of forex investors who use a company is less straightforward. The special provisions that apply to company debts (known as the 'loan relationship provisions') can apply to forex gains or losses on derivative contracts. In this case you would need to assess whether the forex activities were carried out for the purpose of the companies trade.

What is a trading purpose?

A company will have a trading derivative contract if it entered or acquired the derivative contract for the purposes of its trade. So a financial trader that sells or deals in derivatives will enter into or acquire such derivative contracts for trade purposes.

A company will have a non-trading derivative contract if it is not a party to a derivative contract for the purposes of its trade. For example, if:

- it has no trade, such as a pure investment company, or
- as a trading company, it holds derivative contracts for investment or speculative purposes.

Forex gains or losses on forex traders will be taxed as above and all of the profits and losses will be trading profits and losses.

Forex gains and losses on derivative contracts who aren't carrying out a trade (ie investors) will be effectively taxed as interest income in the company (under the special 'loan relationship' provisions that apply to companies). If the expenses exceed the receipts there is then a 'non-trading deficit'.

Note that the profit or loss on the 'investors' activities in the company are treated separately from any trading activities. If there's a profit it's taxed as usual alongside any trading profit, but if there's a loss this non trading deficit is relieved subject to special rules.

Where a company has a non-trading deficit (ie a loss on the derivative activities) it can claim relief:

- against any profits of the company for that period,
- by carry-back against any profits assessable as interest or under the derivative provisions,
- by carry-forward against non-trading profits of the next

accounting period

Note that there is no offset for the derivative losses against any capital gains in the company.

In many cases the derivative provisions won't have any impact on the tax payable though as the receipts will just be taxed as income in the company and any losses would be carried forward against future derivative profits.

Other forex gains/losses

Other forex gains or losses would be likely to be treated as capital gains or losses for corporation tax purposes.

Interest

The main difference will be in relation to interest deductions.

A forex investor will obtain no tax relief for any interest. By contrast a company would have interest deductible as a non trading debit which would reduce the profits. So the fact that the profits are for a non trading use won't prevent there being an offset in the company for interest it sustains.

If you had capital gains on forex in the company the interest payable would still be offset against the forex gains (as the non-trading debit representing the interest would be offset against the gains in the company).

Using a company for forex investing?

As we've seen if the key issue is capital growth (ie you're a forex investor) there are significant advantages to owning personally, particularly if the company has substantial profits and not all of the cash is extracted.

On a disposal of the forex in the future if you own personally you'd be taxed at 18% or 28%. However, if you used a company the tax rate on a future disposal of the company would be likely to be at 20% - 23%. In addition there would still be a tax charge on the extraction of the funds from the company. Any extractions as a higher rate tax payer would incur income tax at an effective 25% for dividends.

There could therefore be a substantially higher tax charge on the disposal of the forex in the company. This is compounded if you then need to extract the cash from the company as a UK resident.

If an existing trading company is used to hold forex an additional problem is that this could result in the company not being classed as a trading company for the purposes of Entrepreneurs Relief, and also inheritance tax.

If you are looking to sell the shares in the company at any point in the future, as a trading company you could qualify for Entrepreneurs Relief to reduce the rate of CGT from 28% to 10% on gains of up to £10,000,000.

This however does not apply where a company has substantial non-trading assets. This includes more than 20% of assets or income in investment assets.

You could therefore run the risk of losing Entrepreneurs Relief on a future disposal of the company if you held forex investments via the company.

It's not just on the sale of a company that Entrepreneurs Relief could be valuable. If for instance you wanted to wind up the company and extract cash etc as a capital distribution, Entrepreneurs Relief could potentially reduce the effective tax rate on the extraction to 10%. If you've had substantial forex investments in the company this would not apply.

Similar provisions also apply for inheritance tax purposes. Shares in a trading company qualify for 100% business property relief (ie excluding the value of the shares from your estate for inheritance tax purposes). If the company has investment assets this could reduce the amount of BPR available.

If the company has substantial investment activities it could raise the rate of corporation tax to 23% rather than 20% due to the close investment company provisions.

There are therefore significant disadvantages particularly in terms of future capital gains in holding via the company.

This would need to be weighed up against the advantages in using a company including:

- The avoidance of the income tax on the extraction of the funds from the company to initially invest.
- The offset of any trading losses in the company against current year gains on the forex
- Using a company can be particularly attractive in terms of interest deductions where you would be classed as an investor.

Overall though if the gains are expected to be significant and you would be looking to extract the proceeds of disposals in the future anyway (and would then incur a UK tax charge on extraction) ownership personally would be preferred to reduce the rate of tax on the actual disposals.

13. NON RESIDENCE & FOREX TAX

Many non resident individuals look to establish whether they are subject to UK tax on the profits from their forex investment and trading activities.

Forex Investors

If they're investors the position is pretty straightforward and they will be exempt from CGT provided they're non UK resident and non UK ordinarily resident for the tax year of disposal.

There are other 'wider' anti avoidance rules that can apply where individuals leave the UK owning the shares/securities and subsequently sell them whilst overseas. In this case they may need to be non resident for at least 5 or 6 complete tax years to get the benefit of the CGT exemption. For departures before 6 April 2013 it is necessary to remain non resident for 5 tax years. This rises to 6 tax years for departures after 5 April 2013.

Forex Traders

If a non resident individual or company is carrying on a forex trade in the UK the position is less straightforward. Whether they are or aren't carrying on a trade is question of fact.

An individual is unlikely to be regarded as trading as a result of purely speculative transactions. For a company, a transaction will generally be either trading or capital in nature.

The active management of an investment portfolio of shares, bonds and money market instruments such as bills, certificates of deposit, floating rate notes and commercial paper does not normally constitute a trade. But every case must be considered in the light of its own facts.

If they are trading in the UK they would then need to assess whether there is a UK permanent establishment or fixed place of business through which that trade is carried out.

The problem here is that brokers and investment managers in the UK could constitute a permanent establishment or a fixed place of business.

The tax legislation though provided specific exemptions for UK investment managers as otherwise they'd be at a disadvantage with other non UK such managers.

Where there is trading in the UK, no assessment is due on the investment manager if the specific exemptions are satisfied. And, except in unusual circumstances (such as where there is a non-financial trade in the UK and the activities are ancillary to that) there is no tax assessment due on the non-resident. Liability is instead limited to tax deducted at source which in practice will be none.

So it all depends whether any investment manager/broker meets the criteria for the exemption. If they do there will be no tax on them/you. If they don't then they would be classed as a UK representative.

Brokers

In order for you to be exempt:

- The broker must be carrying on the normal business of a broker in a market where brokers normally act.

- The transaction must be carried out by the broker in the ordinary course of the broker's business.

- The broker's fee must be at least the customary fee for that class of business.

- The non-resident must not, during the same chargeable period, carry out any trading transactions through the broker other than those which are excluded by this rule.

The purpose of these conditions is to exempt only those brokers who are acting in the ordinary course of their business on arm's length terms. In practice this will cover practically all third party brokers.

Investment managers

The four conditions applying to brokers are mirrored in the conditions which must be met before the exemption for investment managers can apply. These are as follows:

- The investment manager must be carrying on the business of providing investment management services.

- The transaction must be carried out by the investment manager in the ordinary course of the investment management business.

- The investment manager's fee must be at least the customary fee for that class of business.

- The non-resident must not, during the same chargeable period, carry out any trading transactions through the investment manager, other than those which are excluded by this rule.

In addition, the following three further conditions must also be met:

- The transactions must be investment transactions,

- The investment manager must act on behalf of the non-resident in an independent capacity,

- The investment manager must not be entitled to more than 20% of the profit from the transactions on behalf of the non-resident

As for brokers the effect of these conditions is to exempt only those investment managers who are acting in the ordinary course of their business on arm's length terms and are independent of the non-resident.

'Investment transactions' includes transactions in:

- shares
- stock
- securities
- futures contracts (excluding those relating to land)
- options contracts (excluding those relating to land)
- foreign currency
- interest rate, equity and currency swaps
- money placed at interest.

Most financial instruments, including futures and options contracts in physical commodities, are covered by this definition. Spot transactions in physical commodities (including precious metals such as gold bullion) are outside the definition.

So provided your investment manager in the UK meets these conditions you could legitimately trade shares or other financial assets in the UK and be outside the scope of assessment of UK taxes.

14. TAX PLANNING IF YOU INTEND TO BE NON RESIDENT IN THE FUTURE

Speak to many traders and investors and quite a few will be looking to leave the UK in the future. Usually when they've made a large enough profit from their trading or investing activities.

If you you're leaving the UK in the future you'll want to know if there is anything that you could do now (ie whilst UK resident) to reduce your taxes that can take account of the fact you are going to leave the UK in the future?

Well if you're taxed in the UK as a trader on your forex activities one option would be to consider using a company whilst you're in the UK.

If you keep trading in your own name you're going to be subject to the 40% or 45% rate of income tax when your profits (including all your other income) exceeds the basic rate band (currently £32,010 for 2013/2014). You'll also have a 2% NIC charge on profits above this level.

If you trade in your own name and generated substantial profits you'll therefore be subject to these rates irrespective of what you actually do with the profits.

Why not use a company?

One option could be to use a company to carry out the UK financial trade. The UK rate of corporation tax is currently 20% for small companies with profits of less than £300,000.

There would also be no NIC charge on the company profits.

Ideally what you'd then do is retain the profits within the company whilst you are UK resident. The company would use the funds to generate more trades and more receipts.

Then when you leave the UK you can extract the cash. Options here would be to either extract it as a dividend or you could wind the company up and extract as a capital distribution. Both could be free of tax if you're non UK resident.

The net effect of this is that you'd have suffered tax at 20% rather than 42% or 47%.

Here's an example showing you how the figures would look:

Trade in your own name

Lets's say you trade in Forex and generate profits of £100,000 per year. This is your only income.

Your tax bill for 2013/2014 would be:

Income tax:		£
£100,000 - £9,440 = 90,560.00		
£32,010 @ 20% =		6,402.00
£58,550 @ 40% =		23,420.00
Total =		29,822.00
National		insurance:
Class 2 (£2.70 x 52) =		140.40
Class		4:
£41,450 − 7,755 @ 9% =		£3,032.55
£100,000 - £41,450 @ 2% =		£1,171.00
Total		4,343.95

Total income tax & national insurance: £34,165
Using a company

Now lets look at the position using a company. You could actually extract some cash from the company to utilise your basic rate tax band free of any income tax. What you'd probably do is extract a salary of say £7,000. This is not subject to income tax or national insurance.

Corporation tax: £

Taxable profits of company:

£100,000   -   £7,000   =   93,000

Corporation tax £93,000 @ 20% = £18,600

This then leaves £74,400 in the company. You could extract a dividend of £34,450 (gross) to use up the remainder of your personal allowance and basic rate tax band. Assuming you did this you'd have a cash receipt of around £31,000. This would be free of any income tax or NIC.

The remaining cash in the company of just over £43,000 would be retained in the company.

In this year alone you've saved tax of over (£34,165-£18,600) £15,000.

Assume this carries on for 5 years before you leave the UK you would have saved a good £75,000 in UK tax. You'd then have cash in the company of over £200,000. You'd wait until you've established non residence and extract the cash free of UK tax.

Note that it would be essential that you chose your overseas jurisdiction carefully to avoid replacing a UK tax liability with an overseas one (which could be even worse!).

In addition from April 2013 new temporary non residence provisions apply to dividends paid to non-residents from UK close companies. In order to avoid an income tax charge in the year of return the shareholder would need to remain non resident for at least 6 tax years if the dividends are paid from "pre departure" profits.

15. ESTABLISHING TREATY RESIDENCE

OVERSEAS

If you're a trader or investor in forex and are looking to move abroad to avoid UK taxes, establishing treaty residence overseas could certainly make it much easier.

What is treaty residence?

Treaty residence is completely different from the UK's domestic residence requirement. Even if you're classed as UK resident for domestic tax law purposes you can still establish your treaty residence as overseas.

You're classed as treaty resident in a country if you are resident under the applicable double tax treaty.

This will usually apply when you're classed as UK resident and resident overseas under the UK and overseas domestic tax rules.

There are many situations where you could be treated as resident in the UK as well as overseas.

In this case it would be in your interest to look at whether there is a double tax treaty with the UK, and if there is you should look carefully at the residence article.

The residence Article in most modern double tax treaties apply a tie breaker provision (the agreement with the Gambia is one of the exceptions here). This tie breaker clause basically determines in which country a person will be treated as resident for the purposes of the double tax treaty.

The `tie-breaker' rules are basically some tests that are considered one by one until a condition is satisfied. The standard OECD treaty would provide for the tests in the following order:

- **Permanent home.**

An individual is a resident of the country in which he has a permanent home available to him (though not necessarily owned by him). The Revenue will generally look here for evidence of either a freehold or leasehold ownership of land. If you have a permanent home available in both the UK and overseas it is then necessary to look at the next test:

- **Centre of vital interests.**

You will be a resident in the country where your 'personal and economic relations' are the closest. This is a very wide term and means that you'll need to look at where you base your life and regard as your home. So you'll be looking at the location of family, your job, reason for UK visits, location of investments, where your bank accounts are, where you own property etc.

If you can't determine this, you then look at the next test:

- **Habitual abode.**

You'll be a resident of the country in which you have a habitual abode. This is simply the country that you live in for most of the time. If you have a habitual abode in both Countries (or in neither), the final test is to look at:

- **Nationality.**

An individual is a resident of the State of which he is a national.

What difference will this make for forex traders and investors?

The detailed impact will depend on the terms of the relevant double tax treaty - but in essence you get all the advantages of being non UK resident under the tax treaty.

This means that an individual who is 'treaty resident' in another country is entitled to make claims to relief from UK tax as provided for under the tax treaty on the basis that he is a `resident of' the other country.

Most financial traders and investors who go overseas will look to do so to avoid UK tax on the profits and gains from selling the forex etc.

Investors

Most double tax treaties will state that the country of treaty residence has sole taxing rights over gains.

Therefore if you leave the UK and look to sell UK financial assets free of CGT it's clearly essential that you are non UK resident.

However even if you were resident under the terms of the UK's domestic law, providing you're treaty resident overseas the terms of the treaty could apply to ensure that there is no UK CGT charge.

Therefore by establishing treaty residence overseas investors obtain additional certainty in terms of establishing a CGT exemption.

Traders

Most double tax treaties provide that the profits of a trade carried on in the UK is only taxed in the UK to the extent that there is a permanent establishment. Most financial traders wouldn't have a permanent establishment in the UK, and therefore for all intents and purposes the treaty applies to ensure that the profits are taxed solely overseas.

Therefore by establishing treaty residence abroad traders can ensure that profits from the trade are not subject to UK tax.

Out of the frying pan & into the fire

What is essential though is that you carefully pay attention to the overseas tax position. To take advantage of the treaty residence provisions you clearly need to move overseas to a country with which the UK has a double tax treaty.

You'd need to therefore find a treaty partner who taxed the income or gains more favourably than the UK's rules. Countries such as Malta and Cyprus would be good options for financial traders and investors.

Note that treaty residence applies only for the purposes of the tax treaty. So even though you may be resident for the purposes of the tax treaty overseas, if you're still a UK resident under domestic tax law you'll still have to complete UK tax returns.

So, if you're going overseas to a country that has a double tax treaty with the UK, establishing your treaty residence there should always be considered.

This usually means establishing your permanent home there, as even if the UK tax authorities were to argue that you were UK resident under domestic law, if you're treaty non resident you can then apply the treaty provisions as a non resident and potentially avoid CGT and income tax.

16. WHEN CAN YOU BENEFIT FROM OFFSHORE FOREX?

For most UK residents whether they trade in forex via a UK or overseas account, the UK tax position will be the same.

UK residents are usually subject to UK income tax and UK capital gains tax on their worldwide income and gains. So whether they have profits in the UK or the IOM for instance they would still be subject to UK tax.

The main exception to this is in relation to UK residents who are also non UK domiciled. These individuals can choose to be taxed on either the arising basis of tax or the remittance basis of tax.

The arising basis of tax means they'll be subject to UK income tax and capital gains tax just the same as other UK residents.

However the remittance basis of tax means they'll only be subject to UK income tax/capital gains tax on overseas income or gains to the extent that they actually remit the income or proceeds back to the UK. So provided they keep any proceeds overseas they could avoid UK tax investing in forex overseas.

Trading v investing

Note that you need to be careful that you're not classed as carrying out a forex trade from the UK. If you are then the profits will be taxed even if the broker/account is overseas.

Instead you would be looking to be taxed on the basis of being an investor with overseas asset disposals. Most individuals buying and selling forex will be treated as investors for tax purposes anyway.

Who can qualify?

You need to be a non UK domiciliary to qualify.

There are two main types of UK domicile:

- A domicile of origin which is given to you at birth and based on your parents domicile, and

- A domicile of choice where you can choose a new domicile

If you're living in the UK and claiming to be a non UK domiciliary the chances are you'll have been born to parents who were also non UK domiciliaries (or with at least a Father who was a non UK domiciliary if your parents were married).

What are the drawbacks?

The main drawbacks to making a claim for the remittance basis are:
- You would lose the benefit of the UK personal allowance (for income tax) and the annual CGT exemption (for capital gains), and

- After you've been UK resident for 8 tax years you'll be subject to a special £30,000 tax charge on your overseas unremitted income and gains.

It's this latter disadvantage that is the biggest problem. This £30,000 tax charge only makes claiming the remittance basis favourable if you have overseas unremitted gains of over £176,000.

Note though that the £30,000 charge is only an issue after 7 years of UK residence. For the first 7 years you can claim the remittance basis and only lose out by forfeiting the UK tax allowances. This could prove very attractive for any non doms coming to the UK as it gives them a 7 year 'honeymoon period' during which they could retain gains overseas and avoid UK tax.

How do I claim it?

If you are a non dom and you want to claim the remittance basis you'll do this via the self assessment return. The non resident supplementary pages will need to be completed. You won't though need to enter details of the capital gains if you're retaining the proceeds overseas.

Currency pairs and Offshore tax planning

Anyone trading/investing forex will be familiar with the concept of currency pairs.

From a tax perspective irrespective of whether the currency pair is a sterling based currency pair or a non-sterling based currency pair it should still be treated as an overseas asset.

This is an important point for UK tax purposes.

Sterling itself isn't an asset for capital gains tax ('CGT') purposes, instead it's the consideration used to purchase other assets. So effectively you're buying and selling the foreign exchange for UK CGT purposes.

As we've seen above if you're UK resident and domiciled whether you invest or trade in UK or overseas assets will often make little difference. You'll still be subject to UK tax on your worldwide income and capital gains. So whether you bought and sold UK property or forex the capital gain would be calculated in the same way.

However, when you're looking at offshore tax planning, investing in offshore assets such as forex can have advantages.

The first occasion it can be advantageous is for non doms. As we've seen above they can claim the remittance basis for tax purposes and avoid tax by retaining the proceeds overseas.

The other benefit is in terms of non residence.

If you are planning on becoming non UK resident and are classed as a forex trader, dealing in overseas 'assets' such as forex has some significant UK tax advantages. A non UK resident carrying out a UK trade is still within the scope of UK income tax even though they may be non UK resident.

However, if they can establish an overseas trade a non UK resident would be outside the scope of UK income tax. Therefore profits that arise from an overseas forex trade would be free of UK income tax.

Therefore forex traders are in a very beneficial tax position as they could emigrate and avoid UK taxes completely.

Provided they were careful as to their choice of overseas destination they could also ensure that they avoided overseas tax as well.

The location of a forex trade should be taken to be the location of the key revenue generating activities. So unlike the CGT position above it's not determined solely by the forex being an overseas asset, but instead where the forex trader carries out their trade from.

Therefore if they're non resident and making their buy/sell decisions from overseas this would be an overseas trade and exempt from UK income tax.

Unless you're located overseas in a tax haven that has no tax treaties, overseas traders are likely to be subject to the terms of relevant double tax treaties.

Most double tax treaties will only charge an overseas trader to tax in another country if they operate in the other country via a permanent establishment. This is commonly defined as:
' a fixed place of business through which the business of an enterprise is wholly or partly carried on'.

Therefore an overseas trader would in these cases only be taxed in the UK if they had a fixed place of business in the UK. As forex traders wouldn't have any business operations in the UK there would be no UK tax charge under the tax treaty in any case.

Non resident forex investors

Overseas forex investors would be also be outside the scope of UK capital gains tax. However, this is not dependent on the location of any trade or on the forex being an overseas asset. Non residents are exempt from CGT on both UK and overseas assets anyway.

The main caveat to this is that if forex was held as a long term investment and was held at the date of the departure from the UK, the non resident would need to remain overseas for more than 5 complete tax years to avoid the CGT charge arising in the tax year of their return.

Summary

The overseas nature of forex can lead to some effective tax planning opportunities however it would only be non UK doms and non UK residents that could obtain the key benefits of offshore tax planning using forex.

How Non Dom Forex Investors Will Be Taxed On Remittances

Non Dom traders and investors will often look to retain profits from overseas forex trading activities in an offshore account. Providing they claim the remittance basis they will then avoid UK income/capital gains tax on their overseas forex activities.

The problem will be when they look to remit the overseas capital gains back to the UK. If they're UK resident they'll then be taxed on the overseas forex gains.

Reinvesting profits

Most forex investors who take advantage of the remittance basis will look to reinvest forex profits into more forex trading activities. Providing they retain the proceeds and the trades overseas there would be no tax charge.

However when they do look to return profits to the UK they'll need to assess exactly what profits have been remitted.

In particular the tracing provisions can apply to trace the 'original' income and gains through any series of subsequent investments or transactions. This will also include tracing income and gains through other individuals (eg close family members as well as other individuals who then allow close family members to benefit).

So even if you used overseas forex profits to reinvest in an offshore bond and then extracted capital withdrawals from the offshore bond, these capital extractions could be taxed as the previously untaxed overseas forex profits.

Character of the income/gains

Overseas income and capital gains retain their original character. So income remains income and capital gains remain capital gains. The fact that original income is invested so as crystallize proceeds in the future will not prevent the remittance of the proceeds crystallizing income, and not gains. This ensures that untaxed foreign income (potentially taxed at 47%) cannot be transferred into capital gains which would be taxed at 28%.

So you claim the remittance basis on overseas dividend income and then reinvest this into forex investments without a remittance of the forex profits being taxed as income and not capital gains.

Giving away overseas forex profits

It's often asked whether you can give your overseas forex profits for them to bring into the UK. If you're careful to ensure that 'relevant individuals' (essentially close family members) as well as connected companies and trusts don't receive income /gains or benefit in any way you can generally ensure that you avoid there being a remittance.

If though you give untaxed foreign forex gains to another person you should ensure the recipient is aware that they must tell you if the property or anything subsequently derived from it is bought to the UK in circumstances such that there would be a remittance.

How much is remitted?

In practice this is an important point. The amount classed as remittance (and therefore taxable) isn't the value of any assets that are brought back into the UK.

So if for instance you had overseas forex gains equivalent to £50,000 and you then used this to purchase a car which was valued at £30,000 on remittance the amount classed as remitted to the UK would not be £30,000.

The taxable amount is the amount of foreign forex gains from which the property or service derives, and not the value of the property upon remittance.

This will obviously work either in your favour or not:

- If you have an item of depreciating value (such as a car) that is brought to the UK the amount that is classed as remitted isn't the current value of the car but the amount of foreign forex gains from which the car derives. So you would end up with a situation where the amount remitted exceeded the value of the asset actually brought back to the UK.

- If you have an item of appreciating value (eg a work of art) that is brought to the UK, the amount remitted is again the amount of foreign forex gains from which the property derived, and not its current market value. Therefore the asset that was brought back into the UK would be worth more than the actual amount remitted.

Here's a couple of examples to illustrate the key points:

Example

Gordon is a non UK domiciliary and invests in overseas forex. He uses some of his forex gains to buy a painting for £120,000 which is retained overseas. He then sells the painting and uses this to buy some diamonds which are also kept overseas. Ten years later the diamonds are brought back into the UK. This would be classed as a remittance of £120,000 as the diamonds are indirectly derived from his unremitted forex gains.

Example

Gordon used £40,000 of his overseas forex gains to buy a car overseas. The car is classed as being derived from unremitted forex gains. He retains the car overseas and then gives it to his Daughter who brings it into the UK. Gordon remains UK resident/non UK domiciled. At the date of bringing the car back to the UK it is valued at £20,000.

Gordon's Daughter is a relevant person and when she brings the car back to the UK this is classed as a remittance by Gordon.

The amount remitted is still £40,000, that being the amount equal to the foreign gains from which the property (ie the car) is derived.

Example

Gordon also purchased a painting in Italy for £50,000. He used his foreign capital gains from forex investments to purchase this. He then gives it to his wife. She keeps the painting overseas for 5 years and then brings it back into the UK.

In the meantime the artist who painted it has become in high demand and the painting is valued at £100,000.

The painting is treated as derived from Gordon's foreign capital gains. As a result of Gordon's wife bringing the painting to the UK Gordon is classed as having made a taxable remittance of £50,000.

Tax Free Capital

For many longstanding UK resident/non UK domiciliaries traders claiming the remittance basis will not be cost effective as the unremitted overseas income and gains would not make paying a £30,000 remittance tax charge worthwhile.

Remember though that this is an annual charge and should be looked at each year. So if you had a substantial gains on overseas investments in one year which was unlikely to be remitted to the UK it may make sense to claim the remittance basis in that year.

If the arising basis is chosen - as will be the case for many - this means that any overseas income and capital gains will be taxed when it 'arises' whether it's retained overseas or not. So overseas Forex, CFD, Shares and Futures profits would all be taxed in the UK.

If you've got overseas income or capital gains that you've avoided UK tax on in the past due to the remittance basis any transfer of this to the UK would still be taxed.

So essentially being taxed on the arising basis only applies to the current year. For previous years income and gains which are already subject to the remittance basis, the remittance basis will continue to apply.

This doesn't prevent you from bringing in overseas capital to the UK free of UK tax.

Overseas capital can arise from a number of circumstances. As a guide it can include:

- Cash savings from before you became UK resident
- Inheritances from the UK or overseas
- Capital gains from disposals before you were UK resident
- Genuine cash gifts from family/relatives

The key element to all of these is that the income or capital gain was not subject to UK tax originally. As such there is no UK tax on the transfer back to the UK.

Therefore you could use remit from savings before you were UK resident without incurring a UK tax charge on the remittance whether you were taxed on the arising or remittance basis.

You do need to be careful though to identify whether the cash held overseas is pure capital or not.

As you would have been subject to overseas income tax on the remittance basis after you became UK resident any interest or income generated from the overseas cash after this point would be subject to UK income tax on the transfer back to the UK.

So any interest on the overseas cash would be taxed if brought back to the UK even though the capital would not.

Mixed funds

Where you have a case of overseas capital that has accumulated income after you were UK resident you'd need to look at the mixed fund rules.

Essentially these apply so that any withdrawals from the overseas account are treated as the income first (ie taxable) before the tax free capital is classed as being remitted.

So if you had an account that had £100,000 from an overseas

inheritance which had generated £20,000 interest (total £120,000) any transfers back to the UK would first be classed as income up to £20,000. Once you'd remitted the £20,000 the remaining £100,000 could then be brought back tax free.

If you transferred £20,000 to your children this would have no effect as the first £20,000 you actually brought into the UK would still be classed as the income element.

You could though offset any overseas tax suffered, which would substantially reduce or even eliminate any liability.

Remittances of overseas capital gains

The same rules apply to capital and capital gains. So any remittance is first deemed to be capital gain, until that is utilised, with the rest being classed as tax free capital.

For example, if you had sold overseas shares for £300,000 which crystallised a capital gain of £100,000 any remittance of the proceeds would be classed as the £100,000 gain (taxed at 18% or 28%) before the £200,000 tax free capital could be remitted.

So the general idea is that remittances are classed as:
1. income
2. capital gain
3. then capital

If in the above example you'd generated £30,000 of interest on the £300,000 proceeds (total fund of £330,000) a remittance of £100,000 would be classed as £30,000 income and £70,000 capital gain.

A further remittance of £100,000 would then be £30,000 capital gain and £70,000 tax free capital.

'Pure' capital though is always exempt from a UK tax charge.

17. USING AN OFFSHORE BROKER FOR FOREX TRADING OR INVESTING

Anyone investing in Forex will be looking at reducing their UK tax liabilities if they are UK residents. One of the common questions is whether using an offshore broker can assist in reducing any UK capital gains tax charge.

Well in most cases the answer is no:

UK Resident & Domiciled

If you're UK resident and UK domiciled you'll be subject to UK capital gains tax on your worldwide disposals. So any gains made in the UK, overseas and whether you use a UK or offshore broker would all be subject to UK CGT.

Non UK Resident

In terms of UK tax if you're a non UK resident you should be exempt from UK capital gains tax on any gains that arise on a disposal of the forex in the future. The fact that the broker was offshore should not impact on the tax exemption. Provided you are non UK resident the CGT exemption would apply - even if a UK broker was used (as the CGT exemption applies to UK and overseas investments of a non resident).

Note that this is different to the position if you were a forex trader (in which case you'd need to ensure that your UK broker met the requirements to qualify for the broker exemption).

UK resident & Non UK Domiciled

This will apply predominantly to people who are overseas nationals and who come to live and work in the UK.

The benefits of non dom status is that gains on overseas assets such as shares, forex etc may be taxed on the remittance basis.

This means that any capital gain that is realised when shares or forex is sold is only charged to UK capital gains tax when the proceeds are remitted back to the UK.

This can obviously be very beneficial as it can allow UK resident non doms to invest overseas and avoid paying any UK CGT provided they retain the proceeds overseas.

Overseas assets

In order to benefit from the remittance basis it's essential that you are investing in an overseas asset.

The capital gains tax legislation does lay down specific rules for ascertaining where assets are located (there are also separate rules for inheritance tax purposes).

Unfortunately there is rule in the legislation which specifically states where currency is located. Therefore we need to use the rule that applies for tangible moveable property.

The legislation stated that items of tangible moveable property are located where they are found at any point in time. This applies to all rights and interests over such assets also.

Therefore foreign currency can change from being located in the UK to being located overseas if it is transferred from the UK to overseas.

There is also a specific rule which applies to foreign currency bank accounts. This states that:

If an amount is standing to a customers credit at a bank and the customer is an individual and is a non dom, the foreign currency is situated in the UK if:

- the individual is UK resident, and
- the branch or other place of business of the Bank at which the account is maintained is itself situated in the UK.

The net effect of these provisions is that providing you used an offshore broker and the foreign currency was held and 'traded' overseas there is a good case for it being regarded as an overseas asset.

Foreign Currency Bank Accounts

Debts are assets for CGT purposes. The person holding a debt in the form of a credit balance on a bank account is exempt from CGT on withdrawals from the account/

However, this exemption does not apply where the bank account is not in sterling. This means that amounts deposited in an individual's bank account would be subject to CGT on withdrawal. There is an exemption for money that is held for the purpose of personal expenditure abroad by the individual, their family or dependants.

As from April 2012 legislation will be introduced to amend section 252 TCGA 1992 so that the exemption in applies to all bank accounts held by individuals (and trustees).

Therefore there will be no capital gain on the withdrawal from a foreign currency bank account as from 6 April 2012.

18. MAKING THE MOST OF NON RESIDENCE STATUS

Anyone looking to return to the UK should carefully consider their position in respect of any assets that they own. It's frequently the case that they own shares and other investments standing at a considerable gain. The question then is should they be sold before or after a return to the UK?

Selling prior to a return to the UK

If any assets are sold prior to a return to the UK you'd be looking at taking advantage of the capital gains tax exemption for non residents. If you bought the assets after you originally left the UK or if you've been non UK resident for at least five (or six for departures from April 2013) complete tax years you can simply sell the shares during a tax year of non UK residence and avoid CGT in full.

When did you buy the assets?

In order to avoid the five/six year non residence requirement you would need to have bought the assets after you left the UK. But if you're selling shares that you purchased over a period of time how do you know which shares were purchased prior to and after your departure.

In this case you would need to use the share matching rules. Share disposals are matched with shares that were acquired:

- On the same day
- In the next 30 days
- In the new pool.

Some of these rules are very technical however essentially you should be aware that your share disposals are matched with acquisitions on a LIFO (last in first out) basis.

It should therefore be possible in many cases to ensure that the shares were sold prior to a return to UK residence, and with no capital gains tax charged.

Clearly though the overseas tax position would need to be carefully considered, as if you're a resident overseas they may also levy a tax charge.

Selling the shares after you become UK resident

The important point to note here is that once you become UK resident there is no rebasing of your assets to market value. Many returning expats seem to think that once they become UK resident they'll only be subject to UK CGT on the gain that arose after they became UK resident. This is not correct.

Any disposal after you are UK resident will result in a capital gain based on your original acquisition cost - not the market value when you returned to the UK.

Therefore you could be looking to realise a substantial gain by selling after you become UK resident. Of course this isn't always bead news and you'll have to weigh up the tax in the UK if you're UK resident with the overseas tax if you're non UK resident (assuming you get the UK tax exemption as above).

Selling and buying back

Many investors don't want to let tax dictate their investment decisions and may not want to sell any investments prior to a return to the UK (eg they may then lose out on a future rise in the share price). What they then look to do is to sell the shares, crystallise the gain, and then buy them back.

Whilst this is perfectly legitimate it's essential that you leave a period of 30 days in between the disposal and the buy back. Under the share matching rules as outlined above your disposals will be matched with shares acquired in the next 30 days. Therefore if you don't leave a 30 day period you'll find that there will be no gain that crystallises offshore.

19. USING AN OFFSHORE COMPANY FOR FOREX TRADING OR INVESTING

One of the most common questions we have is whether as a UK resident you can use an offshore company to trade or invest in forex & reduce your UK tax charges.

The big advantage of using an offshore company is:

- A non resident company is exempt from tax on capital gains
- A non resident company is exempt from income tax on profits from an overseas trade.

For forex traders and investors these are very attractive tax benefits as they can completely eliminate any UK tax charges on the investing/trading.

The first issue to assess which should always be considered whether you're an investor, trader, resident or not is where the company is controlled from.

A company is classed as UK resident if it's managed or controlled from the UK. The downside in being UK resident would be that the company would be charged to UK corporation tax on its worldwide income and capital gains. This is just the same as a UK company.

Therefore right at the start you'd need to assess where the control of the company was undertaken. If in the UK then there would be little benefit in using an offshore company. Capital gains on forex investing and profits from forex trading would be charged to UK corporation tax.

If you're UK resident and actually live and work in the UK it's not straightforward to argue that the company is controlled from abroad. HMRC want to see active high level control overseas.

Therefore even if you had nominee directors based overseas the company would be classed as UK resident if they simply acted on your wishes. Overseas directors would therefore need to be independent and actually exercise control.

Note that a distinction needs to be made between high level and low level control. If you actively buy and sell forex you could still continue to do this from the UK.

However in order for the profits to be assessed in an offshore company you'd need the actual high level decisions made overseas.

I've therefore seen cases with an offshore company appointing a UK individual as a self employed trader with an overseas MD controlling the company from overseas. The main issue in this case is ensuring that the UK individual isn't classed as a permanent establishment of the offshore company (see below).

UK trade?

One point that you would need to watch out for would be if there was a UK trade. If the offshore company was investing in forex this wouldn't be an issue. But if it was a trading company the profits of a UK trade earned through a UK permanent establishment would be charged to UK corporation tax.

There would be a UK permanent establishment if there was either a fixed place of business in the UK (eg a UK office) or if there was a UK agent capable of binding the offshore company in the UK.

The agent issue is a complex one and we've looked at this separately in another chapter. There are though specific exemptions for investment managers & brokers in the UK.

Anti avoidance rules

The other main problem with using an offshore company to trade or invest in forex is the anti avoidance rules. These apply to UK residents holding interests in offshore companies and trusts. There are crucial differences in how they operate between forex trader and investors and also UK domiciliaries and non UK domiciliaries.

Forex investors

UK resident shareholders in an offshore company will be charged to capital gains tax in the UK on any capital gains that the offshore company makes. So if the offshore company sells forex and makes a gain of £20,000 this gain would be taxed on you in the UK if you owned all the shares. If you owned 50% of the shares, 50% of the gain would be allocated to you.

There is though an exemption from this rule where you hold less than 25% in the offshore company. There could therefore be a possibility for investors to 'club together' to form an offshore company for CGT avoidance.

There are specific rules for UK resident non UK domiciliaires. If they claim the remittance basis of tax they can apply the remittance basis to the anti avoidance rules. So effectively providing the proceeds in the company is retained overseas there is no allocation of the gain to you in the UK. The downside with claiming the remittance basis is that you would then lose your allowances (the UK personal allowance and annual CGT exemption). Of more concern though

They are subject to the transfer of asset provisions.

Where these apply they can tax the forex trader on the company income.

If for instance you are the shareholder and originally subscribed for the share capital then there is a transfer of assets for this purpose (ie a transfer of cash in exchange for shares.

In order for the provisions to apply you'd need to have the power to enjoy the income. This could apply if you could benefit from the company eg dividends or was able to control the application of the income.

Assuming this was the case in order to avoid the transfer of asset provisions you'd need to argue that the motive defence applied.

This is in point where an individual carries on a business overseas provided the reason for the use of the company was commercial. If the company was formed for asset protection purpose it may therefore apply. If there was an overseas forex trade this could in principle apply however you'd need to clearly establish the forex trade as being overseas. So in this respect you'd need to show the key revenue services being carried out overseas. If you were generating the company profits by trading from the UK this would obviously be difficult.

As for CGT, non doms are subject to special rules so that if you opted for the remittance basis this can also apply to the company income attributed under the transfer of asset provisions (ie provided its kept abroad there would be no tax under the remittance basis). If though you're opting for the arising basis of tax you'd need to carefully assess the impact of the above rules as you'd be taxed as another UK resident.

So just who can use an offshore forex company?

Well you'd need to establish control overseas for a start.

Non Doms can avoid UK tax if they're subject to the remittance basis. For other UK residents you're looking at it being a good option for CGT avoidance if you own less than 10% of the shares.

If you're trading, then you'd need to either have purchased an overseas forex trading company or if you subscribed for it you'd need to argue there was no tax avoidance motive.

Remember though that all of this applies just for the company income/gains. In any event if you're UK resident (& domiciled) any dividend from the offshore company would be subject to UK income tax.

20. USING AN OFFSHORE FOUNDATION FOR FOREX TRADING OR INVESTING

Offshore foundations are argued by some to present highly effective tax planning opportunities. In this chapter we look at financial investors and whether they can use an offshore foundation to avoid capital gains tax on forex.

What is an 'offshore foundation'?

In essence it is a special form of trust, however, this simplification does not do it justice.

It s really a cross between a trust and a corporation, and falls into the gap between the two. It is distinguished from a company as it is not the legal personification of a person or group of people, and is instead a legal entity that does not have any owners (shareholders, members or partners).

The assets of the foundation take on a separate legal identity from the personal assets of the participants of the foundation (these can include the Founder, Protector, Council, or Beneficiaries)

Foundations are useful because they are a true separate legal personality. Therefore when applying for an offshore bank account, it is often necessary to state the beneficial owners. If a foundation is used - it is the foundation itself that is the beneficial owner.

Anyone who sets up a foundation can still benefit by being one of the beneficiaries.

Transfer of assets to a foundation

For anyone looking to transfer assets to a foundation this will be treated as a disposal for CGT purposes, just as a transfer to any other corporate vehicle. Therefore the market value rule would apply and the disposal proceeds would be deemed to be the market value of the assets at the date of the transfer to the foundation.

So if you transferred shares or forex into the foundation any gain to date would be charged to UK CGT if you were a UK resident domiciliary.

If you were a non UK domiciliary you could transfer overseas shares into the foundation free of capital gains tax provided you claimed the remittance basis.

The key issue for many though will be the tax position on a disposal of any investments by the foundation…

Gains on disposals by the foundation

One of the key advantages for anyone looking at using an offshore trust or company would be that it would be exempt from UK capital gains tax on any disposals.

Providing an offshore company or trust is non resident and selling UK investment assets it would be exempt from CGT on the gain – at least until April 2015 (we are awaiting details of the proposed changes to the tax treatment of non UK residents selling UK residential property).

Of course this is a pretty straightforward tax planning technique and HMRC therefore have a number of anti avoidance rules to combat this.

There are principally two key anti avoidance rules which could apply to the offshore foundation.

Trust anti avoidance rules

There are specific rules which can attribute gains that arise to offshore trusts to UK beneficiaries. They can apply where a trust 'settlor' can benefit (or there family can benefit) or where a beneficiary receives a capital payment from the trust.

Though it will depend upon the type and terms of the particular Foundation created, as well as the law of the jurisdiction under which it is formed, the property in the Foundation will probably not be "held in trust" so the Foundation should not be treated as a trust under the general CGT purposes.

For the purposes of the anti avoidance rules though the definition of trust is much wider. Under this extended definition a trust/settlement includes "...any disposition, trust, covenant, agreement, arrangement or transfer of assets ...".

It's likely that a Foundation will fall within this definition of trust so that gains accruing to the trustees of the Foundation will be attributable to and chargeable on the beneficiaries who receive capital payments from the Foundation.

This therefore means that any gains that the offshore foundation made when it sold shares, futures, forex or other assets could be taxed on UK resident beneficiaries. Note that if the beneficiaries are non UK domiciliaries and taxable on the remittance basis they'll be taxed on capital payments that are remitted back to the UK.

Corporate anti avoidance rules

There are separate rules that apply to offshore corporate entities which attribute gains of the company to the UK resident shareholders.

If the offshore foundation is treated as a company for UK tax purposes, these provisions will also apply to attribute capital gains accruing to the Foundation to the shareholders in it according to their respective interests.

On the assumption that the Founder is able to direct that the whole of the assets "in" the Foundation are transferred to him (or provided for his benefit), all of the gains accruing to the Foundation will be attributable to the Founder in accordance with these anti avoidance rules and would therefore be taxed on them.

If the UK founder was a non dom these anti avoidance could also apply but will be on the remittance basis if the non dom uses the remittance basis.

There are therefore two possible charges on the same gain, one under the trust rules and one under the corporate rules. In practice, you'd would expect there to be a charge to CGT on the single gain accruing to the Foundation under one provision only.

The question of priority of charge is not straightforward.

Crucially under the new remittance basis, the corporate anti avoidance rules will apply to charge gains on the disposal of assets situated in the UK on an arising (rather than a remittance) basis.

So in this case, if there are gains arising on the disposal of UK shares it seems likely that HMRC would look to apply the corporate anti avoidance rules.

However where the assets are situated outside the UK (eg forex or overseas shares or futures) it may well be that the trust rules will be used so that tax is charged on the direct beneficiary of the gain.

There are therefore a couple of options for taxing investment gains that arise to offshore foundations, and you'd still need to consider the same anti avoidance rules as for offshore trusts and companies.

ABOUT THE AUTHOR

Lee Hadnum LLB ACA CTA is an international tax specialist. He is a Chartered Accountant and Chartered Tax Adviser and is the Editor of the popular tax planning website:

www.wealthprotectionreport.co.uk

Lee is also the author of a number of best selling tax planning books.

OTHER TAX GUIDES

- **Tax Planning Techniques Of The Rich & Famous** - Essential reading for anyone who wants to use the same tax planning techniques as the most successful Entrepreneurs, large corporations and celebrities

- **The Worlds Best Tax Havens** – 220 page book looking at the worlds best offshore jurisdictions in detail

- **Non Resident & Offshore Tax Planning** – Offshore tax planning for UK residents or anyone looking to purchase UK property or trade in the UK. A comprehensive guide.

- **Tax Planning With Offshore Companies & Trusts: The A-Z Guide** - Detailed analysis of when and how you can use offshore companies and trusts to reduce your UK taxes

- **Tax Planning For Company Owners** – How company owners can reduce income tax, corporation tax and NICs

- **How To Avoid CGT In 2013/2014** – Tax planning for anyone looking to reduce UK capital gains tax

- **Buy To Let Tax Planning** – How property investors can reduce income tax, CGT and inheritance tax

- **Asset Protection Handbook** – Looks at strategies to ringfence your assets in today's increasing litigious climate

- **Working Overseas Guide** – Comprehensive analysis of how you can save tax when working overseas

- **Double Tax Treaty Planning** – How you can use double tax treaties to reduce UK taxes

Printed in Great Britain
by Amazon